SPENDING A PENNY

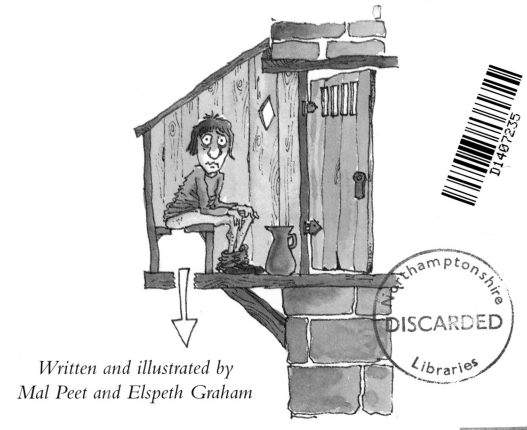

Written and illustrated by
Mal Peet and Elspeth Graham

Collins Educational
An imprint of HarperCollinsPublishers

The Romans built good lavatories, which were often kept clean with running water. There are places where you can still see Roman lavatories which were built two thousand years ago. This is a soldiers' lavatory in a Roman fort.

The Romans didn't have toilet paper. They used sponges tied onto sticks.

The wooden seats were above a channel of water which ran into the river.

The Romans ruled Britain for 400 years. After that, people didn't bother to build decent lavatories.

What do you think these are, then?

It was another 1,500 years before people began building lavatories as good as the Roman ones.

700

years
ago

This is what they looked like inside.

They emptied straight into the moat...

4

Old London Bridge had lots of houses built on it.

Many of these houses shared a privy. Some privies may have had as many as ten seats.

And they emptied straight into...

...the river.

400 years ago

Elizabethan towns stank.
So did most people.

There were no indoor toilets. People used **chamber pots** or buckets and emptied them into the street. It was against the law to do this, but people did it anyway.

Outdoor toilets were usually smelly little sheds. Inside, there was just a wooden seat above a hole in the ground. The Elizabethans called this kind of toilet **the jakes**.

It wasn't just ordinary houses that were smelly. Rich people's houses were smelly too. Even Queen Elizabeth's palace was smelly.

The Queen had a godson called Sir John Harington. He invented the **water closet**, or w.c., a toilet that was flushed clean by water.

The water was kept in this cistern...

...and went down this pipe.

The shell covered up the hole when the toilet wasn't being used.

Most families were too poor to afford a water closet and they didn't have pipes to bring water into their houses. They had to fetch water from wells. It would have been hard work filling a great big cistern.

And someone still had to empty the bucket into a smelly hole in the ground.

250 years ago

Rich people had fine clothes and plenty to eat. But they still didn't have proper lavatories in their houses.

After dinner, the ladies left the room. Then the gentlemen dashed to get their chamber pots out.

This poor man was the public loo. He had two buckets and a great big cloak.

14

He'd hide people using the
bucket inside the cloak.

The Reverend Henry Moule invented the **Mechanical Earth Closet**. A funnel-shaped box was filled with earth or ash. When a lever was pulled a load of earth or ash shot into the pan and covered up whatever was in there.

Earth or ash goes in here.

pull

16

The Mechanical Earth Closet didn't smell too bad, as long as it was kept in a shed outside. But sooner or later some unlucky person had to empty the pan into a smelly hole in the ground.

In Queen Victoria's time, rich people had very smart lavatories in their houses.

Like the lavatories we have today, they were flushed out with water from a **cistern**, like Sir John Harington's invention. Then they emptied into sewerage pipes under the ground.

Victorian toilets and bathrooms were much more fancy than ours. They had lots of marble and shiny brass and polished wood. Of course, only people with lots of money could afford a toilet like this.

Many ordinary people lived in miserable and overcrowded houses.

Some families had their own privy out in the back yard, but often several families had to share one lavatory.

Some streets had a little building with three or four lavatories in it. This was shared by all the people who lived nearby.

21

50 years ago

Many people still had lavatories outdoors. Your grandparents may remember this from when they were little. Some of these outside loos were just like the jakes the Elizabethans used 400 years ago.

Sometimes the outside toilet was right down at the end of the garden. And that could be spooky...

Oh dear, what can the matter be?
Two old ladies locked in the lavatory!
They were there from Monday to Saturday,
Nobody knew they were there.